B

RECIPES

compiled by
Simon Haseltine

With retro art by
Martin Wiscombe

SALMON

Index

Printed and Published by Dorrigo, Manchester, England © Copyright

The Breakfast 'Cornish' Pasty

A hearty way of eating breakfast whilst on the move, or as a picnic, or whilst at work…

Pastry: 1 lb. white plain flour   4 oz. hard margarine (grated)
4 oz. lard (grated)   Teaspoon Marmite (optional)   Around 5 fl.oz. water
Filling: 4 sausages (good quality – thinly sliced)   4 rashers bacon (lean – cut into strips)
4 slices black pudding (chopped – optional)   4 large mushrooms (chopped)
4 free range eggs   Kidney (chopped – optional)
Rolled oats (good pinch)   Salt and pepper

Make pastry by rubbing the margarine and lard into the flour in a large bowl. Add sufficient water and Marmite and knead for around a minute until an elastic dough, then rest the dough in the fridge for at least half an hour. In the meantime, lightly fry the chopped and sliced sausages, bacon, black pudding, kidney and mushrooms. Add a good pinch of rolled oats and set aside. Roll out the dough and cut into 4 x 8 inch rounds using a suitable plate. Place in the centre of each pasty equal amounts of the filling, then break the eggs into a small pan and lightly scramble – pour over the filling and season with plenty of black pepper and a little salt. Dampen one side of the pastry with water, fold to the other side and press firmly together with your fingers. Then fold each corner and crimp, tucking in the end to seal the pasty. Make a small slit in top of pasty with a knife, brush with milk and bake in a hot oven at 400°F or Mark 7 for 30 minutes. Makes 4 hearty pasties.

Three

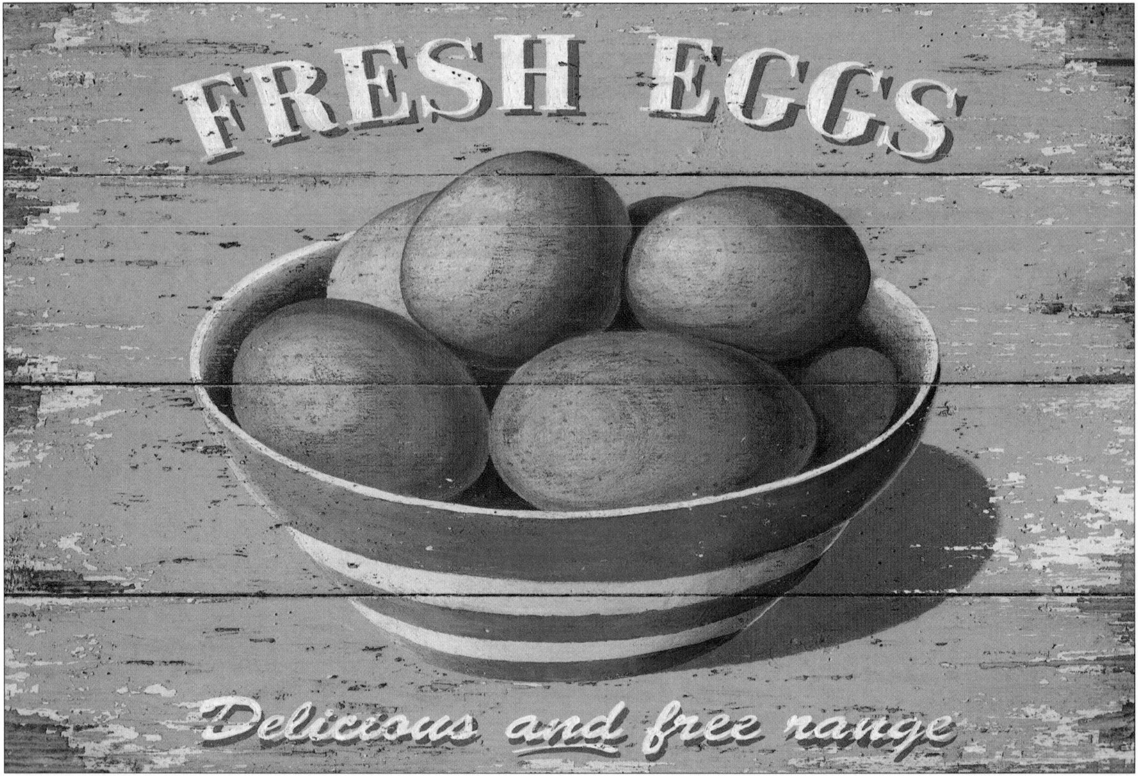
FRESH EGGS
Delicious and free range

Breakfast Omelettes

And with so many fillings to choose from…

Omelette (each):
2 large free range eggs   A little milk
Salt, pepper and nutmeg (grated)   Butter

Selection of Fillings:
Mushrooms (chopped)   Bacon (sliced)   Black Pudding (sliced)
Sliced potatoes (already cooked)   Kidney (chopped)
Tomatoes (sliced)   Chives (chopped)

Grill or fry your selection of filling – ensure a mixture of colour and texture. Scramble eggs in a mug, adding a little milk. Melt a little butter in an omelette pan, pour the egg mixture and add your choice of filling plus a little seasoning. Place lid on pan and cook gently for a few minutes until the egg has just under-set. 'Slide' from pan onto serving plate and fold in half, which will finish cooking the egg. Serve with lashings of baked beans and tomato ketchup.

Good Old English Breakfast

Any recipe book on breakfasts has to include the ultimate in morning cuisine –
the secret is buying the best quality produce from your local butcher and grocer.

Free range eggs (large)   Smoked back bacon
Good quality sausages (try ones like 'whisky and marmalade' which my local butcher makes)
Selection of mushrooms   Tomatoes   Black Pudding
Cooked potato, sliced   Breakfast tea   Toast
Old English Marmalade (thick cut)

Griddle, grill or fry (depending on your diet!) the sausages, bacon, black pudding and tomatoes, and keep warm. Fry your selection of mushrooms in a little butter. Fry the sliced potatoes in a little hot oil, and keep warm. Then poach, scramble or fry the eggs to your liking. Serve with a large pot of English Breakfast tea, followed by some cold chunky toast and marmalade.

Vegetarian English Breakfast

If you can't eat bacon or sausages for religious or vegetarian reasons,
then try this tasty and healthy alternative.

Free range eggs (large)   Large field mushroom (one each)
Beef tomatoes (half each)   Cooked potatoes (sliced)
Vegetarian sausages (plenty of delicious flavours to choose from)
Baked beans   A few Basil leaves

Fry the mushrooms in a large frying pan with butter. Grill the halved tomatoes with the basil leaves. Bring the baked beans gently to the boil. Sauté the potatoes in a little oil. Then, when everything is almost cooked, fry or poach the eggs. Serve, using the large mushroom as the centre piece on the plate.

Scottish Porridge with Honey

*A big bowl of Scottish porridge is certainly the wholesome
and healthy way to start any day…*

Scottish wholemeal porridge oats
Milk and water
Scottish clover honey

For an individual portion, using a normal size mug, measure half a mug of oats into a microwave proof bowl. Add half a mug of milk plus half a mug of water and stir with a spurtle. Microwave on full power for $3\frac{1}{2}$ minutes, stirring every minute. Leave to stand for a few moments before serving. Spoon over lashings of Scottish clover honey, add a little milk and enjoy…

One or two portions can easily be made using this microwave method, otherwise, bring to a boil in a saucepan and simmer for 5 minutes.

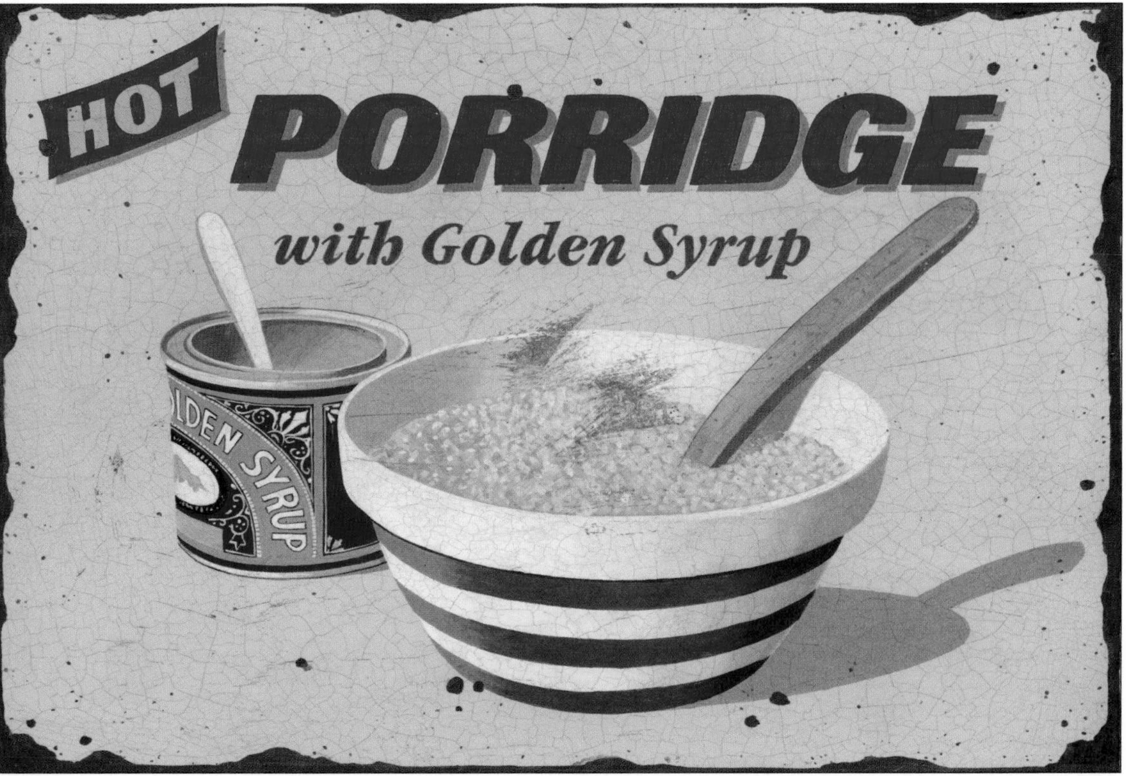
HOT
PORRIDGE
with Golden Syrup
GOLDEN SYRUP

Breakfast Picnic

*If you are travelling and starting your journey early, here are a few ideas
of what to pack for your Breakfast Picnic in the early morning sunshine (or rain!)
half way up or down the motorway*

Small selection boxes of cereal	**Homemade muesli bars or flap jacks**
Freshly squeezed orange Juice	**Breakfast pasty (halved)**
Scotch eggs (halved)	**Breakfast rolls**
Sweet tomato chutney	**Bran scones**

Tubs of yoghurt and some fresh soft fruits

All homemade items are in this book, otherwise pop your selection of
breakfast goodies in a cool box and enjoy your sunny picnic and give the driver
a good rest.

Breakfast Wraps

A modern way to start your day...

A packet of wraps

Selection of fillings:
Scrambled eggs and tomato sauce   Bacon and tomato
Sausage and mushroom   Hard boiled egg, tomato and chives
Scrambled eggs, salmon and chives
Mashed avocado and mushroom, with walnuts

Buy a packet of wraps and let your imagination run riot – cook your selection of fillings, fill the wraps and serve hot with a glass of freshly squeezed orange juice.

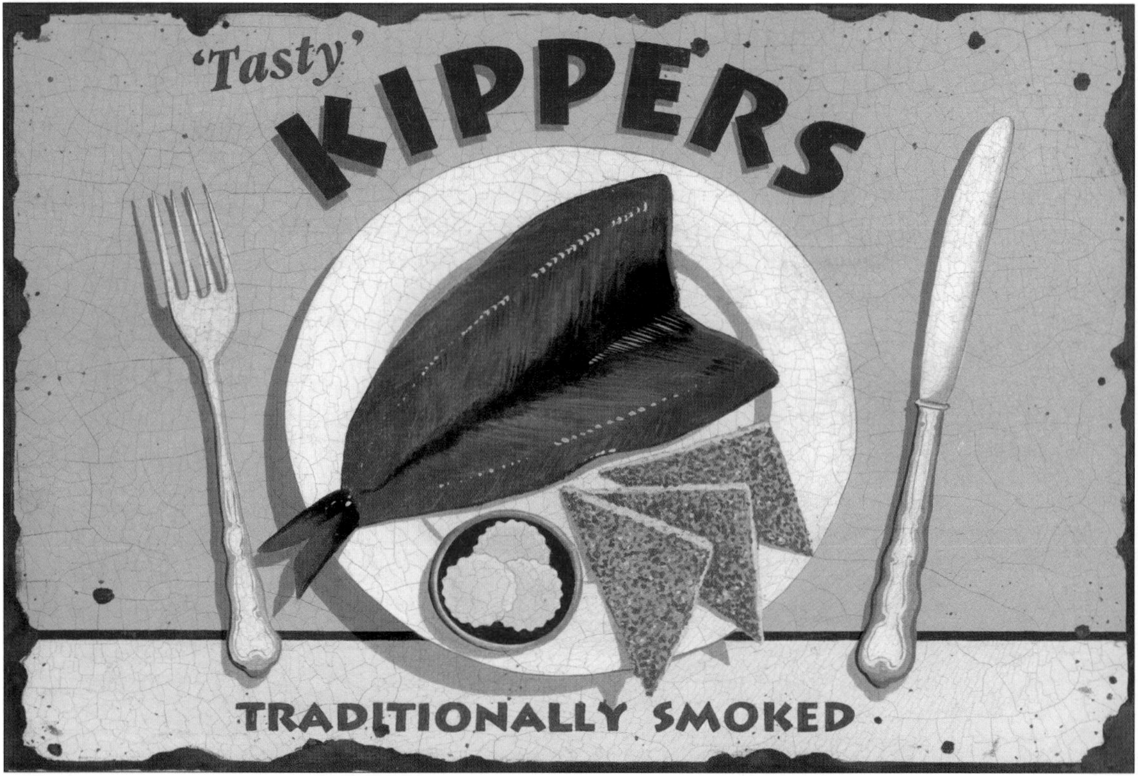

'Tasty'
KIPPERS
TRADITIONALLY SMOKED

Whitstable Smoked Kippers

Whitstable harbour has a wonderful fish market
with locally caught and smoked kippers…

1 smoked kipper each	**Tomato (halved)**
Knob of butter	**Brown bread**
Homemade orange marmalade	

Grill the kipper, skin side up, for a few minutes, until the skin is brown. Turn over, dot with the butter and marmalade, then grill with the tomato for a further 5 minutes, or until golden. Serve with sliced brown bread and a poached egg.

Scotch Eggs

A scrummy breakfast adaptation of this old favourite…

4 small free range eggs (hard boiled) **1 large mushroom (well chopped)**
1 small free range egg (beaten) **Chives (chopped)**
8 oz. sausage meat **Breadcrumbs**
4 rashers bacon (chopped) **Flour for dusting**

Mix the sausage meat, bacon pieces, chopped mushroom and chives, then divide into 4 equal balls. Dust the shelled hard boiled eggs with a little flour and wrap each with a portion of sausage meat. Press the edges firmly together to create a smooth round surface. Coat with the beaten egg and roll in the breadcrumbs. Fry in hot oil until golden brown and serve cold as part of a breakfast platter or picnic.

Sausage and Bean Crumble

Ideal for a frosty winter's morning…

Filling:
8 Sausages   4 oz. Mushrooms   1 tin baked beans   Rolled oats (good pinch)

Crumble:
4 oz. muesli   4 oz. plain flour   4 oz. butter
2 rashers of bacon (cooked and chopped)
Mixed herbs

Brown the sausages, chop and place in an ovenproof dish. Add the chopped mushrooms, oats and baked beans. To make the crumble, mix the flour and muesli together and rub in the butter, then fold in the bacon pieces and herbs. Sprinkle the crumble over the sausage mixture and press down firmly. Bake in the oven at 400°F or Mark 6 for 45 minutes and serve piping hot.

Boxing Day Bubble and Squeak

A festive twist for your Boxing Day breakfast…

Cooked potatoes (roast, new or mashed)
Roast parsnips (chopped)
Cooked chestnuts (chopped)
Cooked vegetables from Christmas dinner
(Swede, sprouts, peas and carrots work really well).
Rolled oats (good pinch)

Mash the potatoes and then mix together with the chopped vegetables, oats and chestnuts. Form into small patties and fry in a little oil until crispy on the outside. Serve hot with a poached egg broken over the top.

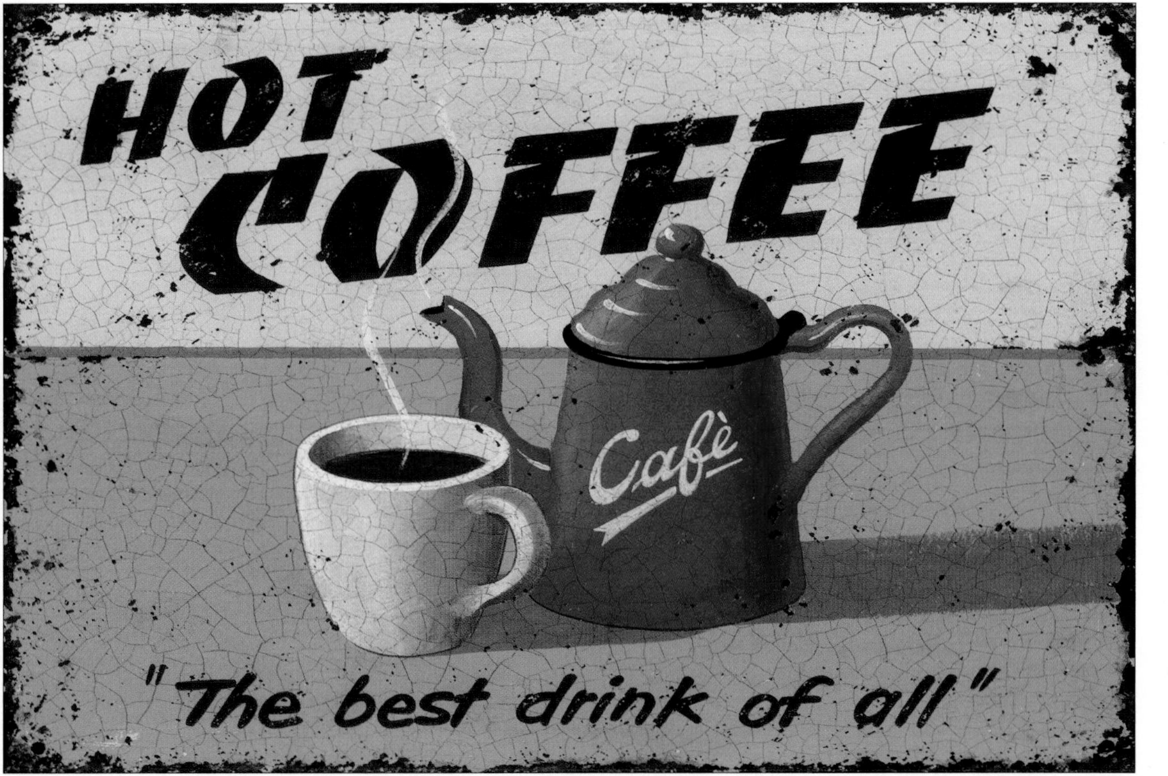
HOT COFFEE
Café
"The best drink of all"

Breakfast Tapas

Fancy breakfast outside in the garden on a warm summery morning, then try this Spanish way to laze away a few early hours of your day…

Ciabatta bread (sliced)	**Ground black pepper**
Plum tomatoes (sliced)	**Basil leaves**
Unsmoked bacon (chopped)	**Olive oil**
Mushrooms (chopped)	**Garlic (optional)**

Fry the bacon, mushrooms and garlic together. Toast the slices of Ciabatta. Crush a tomato over each slice (discard skins), then top with the hot bacon and mushrooms. Add the basil leaves, drizzle with a little olive oil and black pepper and serve with a glass of cold freshly squeezed Spanish orange juice…

Limey Fish Cakes

A tangy start to your day…

4 large potatoes (cooked and mashed)
2 fillets of poached fish such as salmon or haddock (flaked)
Zest and juice from one lime
1 x free range egg (beaten)
A little flour for dusting
Salt and pepper

Fold the flaked fish into the mashed potato, add the egg and lime juice and gently mix together. Season with salt and pepper. Shape into fish cakes and place in fridge for 30 minutes to firm. Dust with flour then fry for around 10 minutes, turning once, until golden. Serve with a poached egg broken over the top.

Bran Scones

The healthy way to keep you going all day long…

1 oz. All Bran	**1 egg**
6 oz. flour	**A little milk**
1 oz. butter	**Pinch of salt**

Soak the All Bran in a little milk. Sieve flour and salt into a basin and rub in the butter until crumbly. Whisk the egg into the All Bran and then add to the dough to form a soft mixture. Knead slightly and place into a small 7 inch cake tin. Score into slices, brush with milk, then bake in a hot oven at 425°F or Mark 7 for 10 minutes. Serve warm with butter or cold on a breakfast picnic.

Kedgeree

My favourite breakfast dish…

8 oz. rice
1 lb. smoked haddock from the fishmonger
4 hard boiled eggs (chopped)
4 oz. butter   A little milk
Parsley   Salt and pepper

Cook the rice. At the sametime, poach the haddock in a little milk for around 10 minutes. Drain the fish and then flake, removing any bones. Drain the cooked rice. Melt the butter gently in a large pan and stir in the cooked rice, flaked fish, 2 chopped eggs and seasoning. Stir for a few moments until well mixed, then serve heaped on a plate with the remaining quartered hard boiled eggs dotted around the base and topped with a sprig of parsley.

Sausage and Mushroom Rice Ramekins

A version of an old recipe my Grandma used to make…

4 sausages (sliced)	**4 large mushrooms (sliced)**
4 oz. rice	**6 fl.oz. water**
1 onion (finely chopped)	**Cherry tomatoes (sliced)**

Cheese (grated)

Brown the sausages and sauté the mushrooms in a pan in a little oil. Drain off excess oil and add the rice and onions, stir and cook for a few minutes. Stir in the water and season to taste, cover and cook gently for 15 to 20 minutes until the rice is tender. Place rice mixture into individual buttered ramekins, sprinkle with plenty of grated cheese, add a sliced cherry tomato and brown under the grill. Serve with fingers of chunky toast.

St. David's Cakes

Celebrate St David's Day with a taste of Wales…

1 large leek (sliced)   **8 oz. self raising flour**
2 oz. Caerphilly Cheese (crumbled)   **2 oz. butter**
4 rashers unsmoked bacon (sliced)   **2 free range eggs**
Pinch of salt

Fry the bacon in a pan for a few moments, then add the leeks and cook for a few more minutes. Allow to cool. Sift the flour and salt into a bowl and rub in the butter until the mixture is crumbly. Then fold in the cheese and bacon mixture. Beat the eggs and add to the mixture and knead into a soft dough. Take 4 lumps of dough and roll each out into a patty. Griddle or fry for 5 minutes each side or until golden brown.

Served with scrambled eggs with a vase of spring daffodils on your breakfast table.

Scrambled Egg with Salmon and Chives

*This is a beautiful way to scramble eggs for a very posh breakfast
when a special friend pops round...*

3 free range eggs each   **Chives (cut)**
Cooked salmon (flaked)   **Salt and pepper**
A little milk

Whisk the eggs with a little milk in a microwave proof bowl. Microwave on full power for a minute, then stir. Continue to cook, stirring every 30 seconds or so, until the eggs are just set. Stir in the flaked salmon and chives, season and serve on some freshly baked chunky toast and butter.

Breakfast Pancakes

Pancakes aren't just for Shrove Tuesday teatime…

4 oz. flour   1 egg beaten   A little salt   6 fl.oz. Milk   Oil

Fillings – scrambled egg and bacon, baked beans and sausage, mushrooms and walnuts, whole frankfurter, bacon and tomato.

Make the pancakes by sieving the flour and a pinch of salt together. Add the beaten egg and combine the milk slowly, whisking until the mixture forms a cream consistency. Heat a little oil in a frying pan and cook each pancake both sides until brown. Place pancakes in a warm oven until all are cooked and the fillings are ready. Place a little filling in each pancake, roll up and serve with lashings of tomato sauce.

Morning Rolls

Nothing beats the smell of freshly baked bread wafting from the kitchen first thing in the morning…

1 lb. strong flour	**A little warm milk**
4 oz. butter	**Packet of yeast**
1 egg	**Rolled oats**

Rub the butter into the flour and add the yeast in accordance with the pack instructions. Break the egg and add a little warm milk into the centre of the flour and stir well together. Cover and set aside in a warm place to rise. Then lightly knead and allow to rise for the second time. Form into small rolls, sprinkle with oats and place on a greased baking sheet, cover and allow to rise again for 10 minutes. Finally, brush with an egg wash and bake in the oven at 450°F or Mark 8 for 15 to 20 minutes until cooked and sounds "hollow" when tapped underneath.

Sausage, Mushroom and Baked Bean Lasagne

Now, here's a tasty surprise – lasagne for breakfast…

8 good quality sausages (sliced)
Closed cup mushrooms (sliced)
2 cans baked beans
4 hard boiled eggs (roughly chopped)
Mixed herbs (pinch)

Tomato puree (a good squeeze)
Rolled oats (a good pinch)
½ pint of cheese sauce
Lasagne sheets (ready to cook)
Cheese (grated)

Salt and pepper

In a large frying pan gently brown the sliced sausages and mushrooms. Drain off any fat and add the baked beans, mixed herbs, tomato puree, rolled oats and egg. Season and stir for a moment. In an ovenproof dish, layer the lasagne sheets and the sausage mixture, finishing with a layer of lasagne. Sprinkle some grated cheese on top and place in oven and bake at 400°F or Mark 6 for around 40 minutes. Serve with a poached egg.

Baked Mushrooms

Use a selection of mushrooms to make this dish unique every time…

100g mushrooms (use a variety)   **A little milk**
4 eggs   **Salt and pepper**

Chop and gently fry the selection of mushrooms. Butter individual ramekins and add the cooked mushrooms. Add a tablespoon of milk into each dish, a little seasoning and then break an egg over the top. Bake in a hot oven at 425°F or mark 7 for around 15 minutes or until the egg has set.

Breakfast Bread and Butter Pudding

Well, if you are going to have a pudding for breakfast,
then it has to be a marmalade sandwich…

14 slices of medium cut white bread	4 oz. icing sugar
6 oz. unsalted butter, softened	2tsp vanilla essence
Jar thick cut orange marmalade	1 pint milk
4 whole medium eggs	Nutmeg
4 medium egg yolks	Demerara sugar, for sprinkling

To Serve:
Dollop of marmalade

Butter the bread (leaving some of the butter) and spread half with marmalade. Make into sandwiches, cut each into 4 triangles and layer in a buttered shallow ovenproof dish. Make the custard by whisking the eggs, egg yolks and the icing sugar together in a large jug. Add the vanilla essence and milk and whisk together. Pour the custard over the marmalade sandwiches and leave to stand for an hour for the custard to soak into the bread. Grate over some nutmeg, sprinkle with demerara sugar and dot with the remaining butter. Bake in the oven at 400°F or Mark 6 for 40 minutes or until the custard has just set and the top is golden brown. Serve the bread and butter pudding with a large dollop of marmalade.

Breakfast Flan

A wonderful way to create a light flan packed full of your favourite breakfast goodies…

For the flan:
6 oz. plain flour   2 oz. Butter   1 free range egg yolk
Pinch salt   A little water

For the filling:
4 rashers unsmoked bacon (cut in strips) (omit for vegetarian flan)
4 small closed cup mushrooms (chopped)
2 firm tomatoes (skins removed and chopped)
3 eggs   ½ pint milk   Salt and pepper

Sieve flour and salt into a bowl, rub in the butter and bind together with the egg yolk and a little water until a soft dough is achieved. Knead and roll out the pastry and line a 7 inch flan ring. Place the bacon, tomatoes and mushrooms into the flan, beat together the eggs, milk and seasoning and pour over the filling. Bake in the oven at 350°F or Mark 4 for around 45 minutes or until the egg has set. Serve cold as part of a breakfast picnic or buffet.

Seasonal Fruit Smoothie

Grab some seasonal fruit and wiz up a scrummy smoothie…

Seasonal Fruit (around 8 oz. fruit per person)
½ banana each – to add body
Milk – for a thinner smoothie
or
Yoghurt – for a full bodied smoothie
or
Apple Juice – for a more refreshing smoothie
plus
Honey to sweeten (optional)

Simply wiz up your ingredients, pour and enjoy. Experiment with different combinations of fruit, quantities and by adding milk, yoghurt or apple juice. You can also add oats or nuts to make a coarser texture.

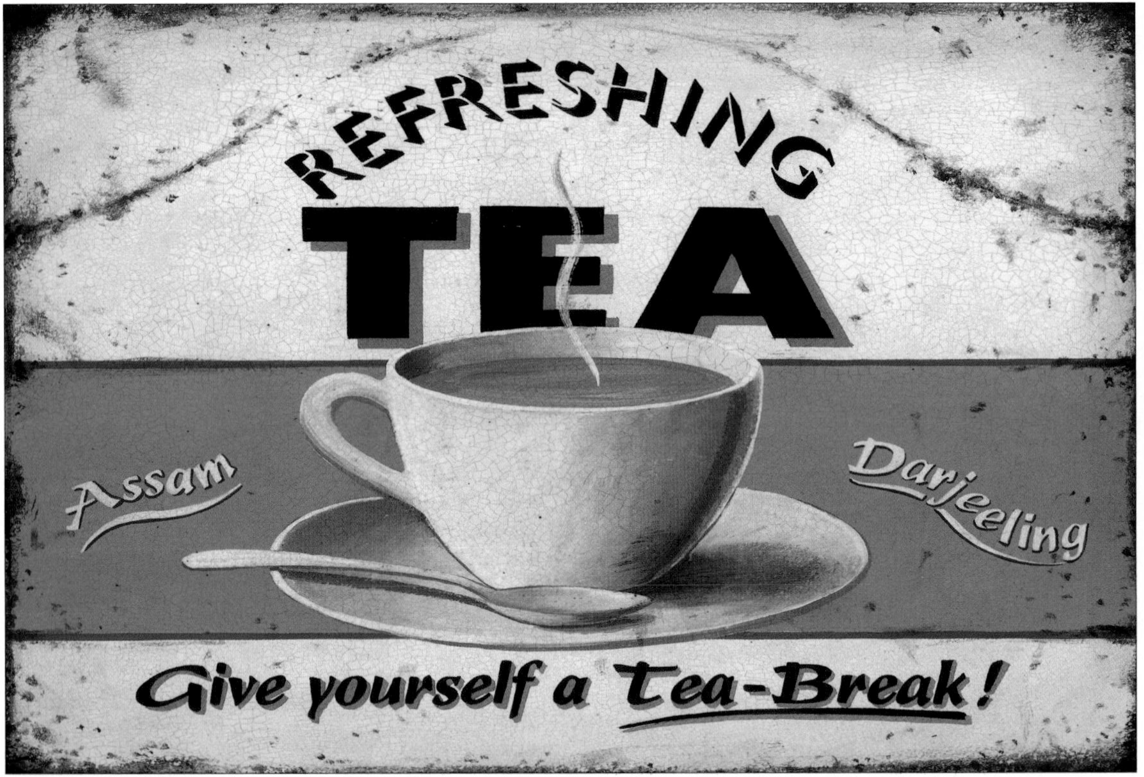
REFRESHING
TEA
Assam
Darjeeling
Give yourself a Tea-Break!

Tomatoes Stuffed with Mushrooms

A colourful morning treat…

For 2 portions:
2 beef tomatoes   1 onion (chopped)
2 rashers smoked bacon (sliced)
2 large mushrooms (chopped)
1 garlic clove   Olive oil   Salt and pepper

Halve each beef tomato, remove the seeds and rub the outsides with a little olive oil and season to taste. Place on a baking tray and roast in a moderate oven for 10 minutes, or until tender. Meanwhile, fry the onion for a few minutes, then add the bacon, mushrooms and garlic and continue frying until cooked. Finally, spoon the bacon mixture into the hot tomato halves and serve with a poached egg.

Yorkshire Breakfast

A scrummy version of this northern hearty delight…

Yorkshire Pudding:
4 oz. self-raising flour
1 large free range egg
½ pint milk

Filling (per person):
2 sausages, chopped.
1 slice black pudding, sliced
1 rasher bacon, chopped.
1 tomato, sliced

Sieve the flour into a bowl and whisk in the egg, then add sufficient milk to make a thick creamy batter. In the meantime, fry the sausages, bacon, tomatoes and black pudding until cooked. Heat a small amount of oil in individual Yorkshire pudding tins until smoking. Then carefully place the filling ingredients into the hot oil and pour over the batter. Place in the oven and cook for around 30 minutes or until the batter has risen and is a golden colour. Serve with baked beans and a poached egg inside each pudding for a truly hearty breakfast…

American Christmas Muffins

Take the delicious American Muffin and add a festive twist…

4 oz. butter, melted	1 tsp bicarbonate of soda
½ pint buttermilk	1 tsp cinnamon
2 eggs, beaten	8 oz. caster sugar
1 tsp vanilla extract	4 oz. cranberries (dried)
12 oz. self-raising flour	A little demerara sugar, for sprinkling

Slowly melt the butter in a pan and mix in the buttermilk, eggs and a little vanilla extract. Sift the flour with the bicarbonate of soda and cinnamon into a large bowl, then stir in the sugar. Add the milk mixture and mix until a soft batter. Stir in the cranberries and spoon into individual paper cases. Sprinkle a little demerara sugar over each and bake in oven at 375°F or Mark 5 for 25 minutes until risen and golden. Serve warm for a Christmas morning breakfast.

English Muffins

The traditional breakfast muffin from an old recipe.

1 cup milk	**1 cup warm water (tepid)**
2 tablespoons white sugar	**¼ cup melted cornmeal**
1 pack active dry yeast	**6 cups all-purpose flour**
	1 teaspoon salt

Gently warm the milk in a small saucepan until it bubbles, then remove from heat. Mix in the sugar, stirring until dissolved. Let cool until lukewarm. In a small bowl, dissolve yeast in warm water. Let stand until creamy, about 10 minutes. In a large bowl, combine the milk, yeast mixture, shortening and 3 cups flour. Beat until smooth. Add salt and rest of flour, or enough to make a soft dough. Knead. Place in greased bowl, cover, and let rise. Punch down. Roll out to about ½ inch thick. Cut rounds with biscuit cutter or drinking glass. Sprinkle waxed paper with cornmeal and set the rounds on this to rise. Dust tops of muffins with cornmeal also. Cover and let rise for ½ hour. Heat a greased griddle or heavy bottomed frying pan. Cook muffins on griddle for about 10 minutes on each side on medium heat. Keep baked muffins in a warm oven until all have been cooked. Allow to cool and place in plastic bags for storage. To use, split and toast. Great with orange butter, or cream cheese and jam. Add grated cheese, fried bacon bits or sun dried tomato to add various delicious flavours...

Forty

Devilled Kidneys

I used to help at a restaurant serving breakfasts many years ago and this was always a popular dish...

2 thick slices crusty bread	**1 tbsp red wine**
2 tbsp olive oil	**1 tsp wholegrain mustard**
2 lambs kidneys, cored and chopped	**2 tbsp double cream**

1 tbsp fresh parsley, chopped, to garnish.

Preheat the oven to 400°F or mark 6. Place the slices of bread onto a baking tray, drizzle with a little olive oil, then bake in the oven for 4 minutes until toasted. Heat the remaining olive oil in a frying pan and add the chopped kidneys. Stir for a few moments to brown, then add the red wine and wholegrain mustard and fry for a few further minutes until cooked. Next add the double cream, heat through for a minute. Arrange the sliced toasted bread onto a plate, spoon the devilled kidneys on top, then sprinkle with the chopped parsley.

Homemade Hash Browns

Try them homemade – you'll never buy shop ones again…

1 egg, beaten   **1 medium onion**
4 medium potatoes   **Salt and pepper**
Vegetable oil for frying

Coarsely grate the potatoes and onion into a clean tea towel and then squeeze out the excess liquid. Empty into a bowl and add the egg, a little salt and pepper and mix well. Make the potato mixture into small flat patties, then fry each in hot oil for around 5 minutes until golden, turning once. Serve hot with your eggs and bacon.

Egg Florentine

The classic of all breakfast dishes…

Frozen spinach (allow 5 oz. each)   **Chunky toast**
Free range eggs (1 each)   **Salt and pepper**

Cook the spinach in accordance with the instructions and drain well. Meanwhile, poach the eggs in water and toast the bread. Serve by placing the spinach on the toast, making a small well in the centre for the egg and season well with salt and pepper.

Potato Breakfast Scones

Simply delicious…

1 lb. of mashed potatoes   4 oz. of plain flour
2 oz. of butter   Pinch of salt

Boil and mash the potatoes, add the butter and a little salt and fold. Then add the flour and mix thoroughly. Form into small patties and roll out to the desired thickness (thin for pancakes, thick for scones). Then fry or griddle for 5 minutes each side, or until cooked and golden brown. Serve hot with a Scottish breakfast…

Morning Flapjacks

Ideal for a healthy breakfast on the move…

2 oz. margarine   1½ oz. light brown sugar
1 tablespoon of golden syrup
6 oz. of porridge oats or your favourite cereal

Place margarine, sugar and the syrup into a saucepan and stir over a low heat until the fat and sugar have melted. Add the oats/cereal and blend thoroughly. Then press into a well-greased 7 inch square sandwich tin and bake in the centre of a moderate oven at 350°F or Mark 4 for 25 minutes or until evenly golden brown. Score and allow to cool.

METRIC CONVERSIONS

The weights, measures and oven temperatures used in the preceding recipes can be easily converted to their metric equivalents. The conversions listed below are only approximate, having been rounded up or down as may be appropriate.

Weights

Avoirdupois	Metric
1 oz.	just under 30 grams
4 oz. (¼ lb.)	app. 115 grams
8 oz. (½ lb.)	app. 230 grams
1 lb.	454 grams

Liquid Measures

Imperial	Metric
1 tablespoon (liquid only)	20 millilitres
1 fl. oz.	app. 30 millilitres
1 gill (¼ pt.)	app. 145 millilitres
½ pt.	app. 285 millilitres
1 pt.	app. 570 millilitres
1 qt.	app. 1.140 litres

Oven Temperatures

	°Fahrenheit	Gas Mark	°Celsius
Slow	300	2	150
	325	3	170
Moderate	350	4	180
	375	5	190
	400	6	200
Hot	425	7	220
	450	8	230
	475	9	240

Flour as specified in these recipes refers to plain flour unless otherwise described.